MOURNING

Finding the Way Forward

MOURNING

Finding the Way Forward

Nnenna Moneme

Unless otherwise indicated, Scripture is taken from the Holy Bible, New International Version®, NIV®. Copyright © 1973, 1978, 1984, 2011 by Biblica, Inc.™. Used by permission of Zondervan. All rights reserved worldwide. www.zondervan.com. The "NIV" and "New International Version" are trademarks registered in the United States Patent and Trademark Office by Biblica, Inc.™.

Scriptures identified as KJV are taken from The Authorized King James Version. Rights in the Authorized Version in the United Kingdom are vested in the Crown. Reproduced by permission of the Crown's patentee, Cambridge University Press.

Scripture quotations marked NLT are taken from the Holy Bible, New Living Translation, copyright ©1996, 2004, 2015 by Tyndale House Foundation. Used by permission of Tyndale House Publishers, Carol Stream, Illinois 60188. All rights reserved.

Copyright © 2022 by Nnenna Moneme

All rights reserved. No part of this book may be reproduced or used in any manner without written permission of the copyright owner except for the use of quotations in a book review.
For more information, email: chiegemoneme@gmail.com

FIRST EDITION

https://youtube.com/user/Angeldozie

978-1-80227-912-2 - eBook
978-1-80227-913-9 - paperback

To anyone who has experienced loss and is finding it difficult to move forward. I'm praying that by sharing vulnerably through my writing, I can point you in the right direction so you can move on from your loss.

To my extended family, friends and church family for helping me move from grieving to living again.

To my husband, Revd Dozie Moneme, for helping me discover my gift of writing and encouraging me to use it to serve others.

ACKNOWLEDGEMENTS

My heartfelt gratitude goes first to my Lord and Saviour Jesus Christ, for teaching me these truths by His Spirit and enabling me to teach others.

I would like to express my immense gratitude to my beloved husband and pastor – Revd Dozie Moneme – who helped me discover my gift and encouraged me to serve others with it. I am eternally grateful for your unending love and support. I love you.

I also wish to show my appreciation to our three lovely children – Chimdiuto, Chukwubuikem and Chizitelu for always sharing their parents with the world. You three bring us so much joy. I pray you will keep growing to love and serve our good Lord. Mummy loves you all.

I would like to thank all of my family (my mum Veronica, sisters Amaka, Ogochukwu, Nkechi and the rest of our extended family) and Christian friends (Ifeoma and Kene Ezeibe, Ifeoma and Chidi Umeaku, Pauline and Kalu Ukariwe, Ifeanyi and Obioma Onunkwo, Samson and Oge Egbuluonu, Sunday and Edit Okereke, Kabia Blessing Gbirigbe, Emeka and Onyekachi Okechukwu, Abiodu and Tolu Alonge, Ngozi and Udy Anya, Chyke and Uche Ohuegbe, Nana and Emma Ikenma), for speaking words of comfort and sending practical help that made the path to recovery a lot easier than it otherwise would have been.

Last but not least, to my beloved sisters from our current local church family – Margaret Norris, Liz Day and Josephine Hinson. Thank you for organising and editing my writing and supporting me in bringing this work to fruition. God bless you all.

CONTENTS

Chapter 1 - The Pain of Loss 1

Chapter 2 - The Struggle to Move Forward 5

Chapter 3 - A Different Perspective 9

Chapter 4 - Moving Forward 15

Chapter 5 - Honest Conversations... 25

Chapter 6 - The Ultimate Loss 33

Chapter 7 - Graduation Ceremony 37

About the Author 41

Chapter 1

THE PAIN OF LOSS

"Men, I can see that our voyage is going to be disastrous and bring great loss to ship and cargo, and to our own lives also." Acts 27:10.

"Have you seen my glasses?" I asked my husband frantically.

"No. Where did you put them?" he questioned.

"I left them on top of the table," I replied with a tone that portrayed I was deeply stressed. I didn't care what anyone thought at that point; all I wanted was my glasses, and immediately! I depend on my glasses because they allow me to live a normal life, so losing them was a real discomfort. As I searched each room, my emotions took over. I became tearful and unwilling to listen to anything other than ideas of where my glasses could be, and finding them was the only thing that could calm me down.

Sure, most people will agree that losing something little like a car key, bank card, a small amount of money or your glasses (as in my case) can take a toll on our emotions. This minor emotional disruption feels like child's play when we are dealing with bigger traumas like the death of a loved one, the loss of our health or home or a threat to our survival, such as a job redundancy.

Besides losing my glasses, I recently faced a deeper crisis while dealing with the Coronavirus pandemic. As a health worker, I had to work while others stayed home. At the beginning of the pandemic, going to work was far from normal due to the constant thoughts and fear of acquiring the virus. As patients trickled in, facing them was not the same because they were not just patients but potential carriers of the virus. My mind raced every day with thoughts like: "What happens if I contract this virus and pass it on to my husband and the children? Or worse still, what if I then deteriorate and go to heaven, leaving only my husband to carry the burden of caring for our young children as well as running the ministry?" I prayed hard for myself and my colleagues.

In these early stages, as I prayed, things appeared to get worse. In the hospital where I work, our department is situated opposite the mortuary. Soon, the mortuary was full, and the next department had to be used as an overflow. To challenge my mental health even further, while walking into work one morning, I witnessed yet another person's loved one being taken to the mortuary. I tried to put it out of my mind and went to work as usual. I opened my emails, and one message advised that a colleague had just died from the virus. Although I kept trying to be an encouragement to other staff at work, the truth was that I was also battling negative thoughts. These inner feelings made me realise that no matter how spiritual a person may be, losses are real and can paralyse our emotions in ways we could never imagine. Like the biblical character Job, who had sequential losses, we can turn from being full of joy and laughter to mourning, grieving and even having a desire to die. I am sure we all feel some of these emotions at times, regardless of whether we experience small or more significant losses. The pain we feel can lead us to mourn, and these emotions can cause us to lose direction. Like people groping in the dark, we may begin to wonder which direction can lead us back to the light.

Imagine how Paul and the men in his ship must have felt in the life and death situation described in Acts Chapter 27, verse 10. They were about to face a storm that would not just cause the loss of goods but might also cost their lives. Like with these men, our own life may be moving towards the pending danger of possible loss because our loved one is battling a recently diagnosed life-limiting illness.

Perhaps you are not dealing with a loved one's pending death; rather, you have lost someone dear to you, like your spouse of many years, a child or even a close relationship that has deteriorated and you have now parted. Losing these precious life support systems can leave us feeling deep pain that, if not properly processed, we may never recover from. I remember my 48-year-old dad battling cancer for five years and finally dying on a theatre table. After his demise, our family were informed that when the doctors took him to the theatre to fix a colostomy bag, he bled so much that he lost his life in the process. I was away from home when this happened. My dad had dropped me off at the bus station before I'd travelled. He reassured me the surgery would happen when I was home. Unfortunately, the surgery was rescheduled, and Dad's surgery had to be done before I arrived. Coming home and realising my dad had died left a deep pain in my heart that was difficult to process until I discovered, from God's Word, some of the truths I will share with you in this book. Both my dad's death and the death of my best friend seven years later took me on a journey of learning how to move from deep pain to recovery, finding the right path to allow me to live again without being stuck in the difficult feelings of my bereavement. I do hope you read to the end of this book and apply these truths in your own life, as well as share them with someone else who may be struggling to move forward from their loss.

Chapter 2

THE STRUGGLE TO MOVE FORWARD

"From the ends of the earth I call to you, I call as my heart grows faint; lead me to the rock that is higher than I." Psalm 61:2.

As David described in the psalm above, a loss generates an overwhelming feeling that can leave us struggling and stop us from moving forward. As well as losing my dad in my teenage years, I also lost my best friend suddenly while we were eating a meal together shortly after we left university. With both losses, I realised that even though the burial was over, the pain and grief can remain fresh and unrelenting for months and sometimes years if the grieving process is not properly managed.

Although these two tragic losses were seven years apart, the constant fear that gripped me was inexpressible for each experience. First, I was terrified that sudden death might befall another of my loved ones. The constant thought that someone else would die, even if they only had a headache, strongly influenced my thought patterns. My dad was sick for five years before he passed away. Those years of sickness helped us prepare for his death. However, the sudden death of my friend was something I had never experienced and was a difficult pill to swallow.

Apart from this constant anxiety, there were many other unvoiced struggles deep within that needed addressing before they took a firm hold of me. I feared I might never find someone to build a friendship and support system with like the ones I had shared with my friend and my dad. Everything about the future appeared bleak and scary, and facing it felt like a scattered puzzle that needed time to fit together. How could I process all these emotions, put the past behind me and begin to move forward without getting stuck in my grief?

I was not afraid of being alone because I was a Christian and had already built a personal relationship with Jesus Christ before these losses. I believe having this foundation stopped me from degenerating into a state of despondency or deep depression. The challenge was that losing someone like my dad meant that all I had depended on him to do was now difficult to navigate. I remember having to complete countless pieces of paperwork after each episode of bereavement. As I opened each envelope and read through its contents, I kept holding back the tears that flooded my eyes. Thankfully, my mum was around on such occasions to ensure I was okay. She spoke softly in the background while watching me cry.

"You know, once you bury the dead, they are not coming back here. Rather, we will go like they did one day," she said gently. "You have to realise that Dad is dead now and thank the Lord for the years you shared, then move forward," she emphasised further.

Move forward mum? Move forward? "Tell me how I can move forward when I cannot see Dad any longer," I cried and lamented at the same time.

"Yes, he is not here, but God allowed it, and you have to trust Him to help you accept your loss and move forward. We are in a better position than most people because we know our loved one is in heaven. You know what the Bible says about Christians when they die: 'absent in the body is present with the Lord,'" mum reminded me. "I know it is not easy. However, you must never allow yourself to be stuck in grief. You need to make gradual progress refusing to blame or regret. Take it one day at a time, please," she clarified further.

I knew exactly what my mum was saying because we have encouraged the bereaved by quoting this Scripture in 2 Corinthians 5:8: "We *are confident, I say, and would prefer to be away from the body and at home with the Lord.*" I knew this truth, and I believed it, but pain and grief are real no matter how much you believe the truth of God's Word. This was a season of mourning and grieving. I needed time for the wound to heal, and I could not rush it. Like mum said, it's one day at a time. Slowly but surely, I went through the stages of grief, which ended in acceptance. Until this was done, I was not ready to move forward. This is not uncommon. Many are stuck in their grief, often recounting their sad loss for many years without making the required progress of putting the past behind and moving forward. The truth is that God wants you healed and recovered so that you can live again without being held in this challenging period of your life. With this in mind, I will encourage you to consider applying the biblical principles I will share in the next two chapters.

Chapter 3

A DIFFERENT PERSPECTIVE

"'For my thoughts are not your thoughts, neither are your ways my ways,' declares the Lord." Isaiah 55:8.

Have you ever considered that there may be a different perspective on your loss? Do you realise that God may be working behind the scenes, opening a gateway to another era of blessing and trust that you may never have experienced before? When my husband and I met, he had buried his mum and his only sister the previous year. Both of them died within a space of two months, and their deaths left my husband devastated. He almost gave up, as these were the only female figures in his life. As he grieved their loss, he did not realise that God had gone ahead of him to prepare a wife that he would soon marry. He did not see this blessing coming because he was still stuck in grief. A few years later, after our wedding, he reflected on this and shared honestly with me, saying: *"I am convinced that God sent you and our daughter to console me after these sad losses. I never knew I would ever meet a woman who would take care of me as my mum and sister did."* I simply laughed, reminding him that this is the problem with grief; it blinds you from seeing what God may be planning.

With the sad losses I experienced, it was easy to wallow in self-pity. However, it was not long before I began to see God's hand in my pain. This only happened because I had spent years delving into God's Word: The Bible. The foundational truths God taught me over the years are why the pieces of my life came together until they formed a beautiful tapestry that people admire today. I would love to share some of these life-changing principles with you and hope that you will meet God and feel His comfort personally as you read the rest of this book.

Trusting God for the Future

As described in the previous chapter, fear was one of the main struggles I faced following my bereavements. This was not the same as the shock and fear that is often part of the initial grieving process; rather, this was a constant fear that other, similar tragedies would occur again and again. The good thing was that I knew exactly where to get help. This may sound old-fashioned because, in our day and age, everyone wants more modernised, quick-fix options. However, the old principle of going back to basics is the secret of healing. I returned to my routine of spending time in prayer and reading the Bible, and something miraculous began to happen. First, my eyes fell on this Scripture: *"What do ye imagine against the LORD? He will make an utter end: affliction shall not rise up the second time." (Nahum 1:9, KJV).*

"Affliction will not rise again," I repeated to myself. I had been afraid someone else might die suddenly, and this Scripture assured me that this would not happen twice. Reading this made me feel free. I learnt this Scripture and meditated on it over and over again. I felt so liberated from the fear that had gripped my heart for months. For the first time in a long while, the fear of losing a young member of the family was not present.

There is unexplainable power in God's Word to change our lives. With the awareness that someone may pick up this book without knowing or ever reading the Bible, my suggestion would be to find a quiet place and start reading from the book of John. This book displays the love of God in one of the most inviting ways. If the Bible is not easily accessible to you, use the Internet and try Bible Gateway or other tools that allow you access. I have also added a link to my new believers' study manual at the end of this book, which is available electronically and in hard copy.

Another day, I was studying the scriptures and read Isaiah Chapter 55. While reading, I felt the Lord emphasise in verse 8 that my thoughts were not His thoughts. After witnessing my friend die at 29 and my dad at 48 years old, I started doubting the promise of a long life, which the Scripture clearly shows as God's gift to us if we walk in His ways. *Psalm 91:16 (KJV) says: "with long life I will satisfy him and show him My salvation."* My heart ran through several scriptures as I meditated on God's Word. I realised that many people who had walked with God, like Abraham, Isaac, Jacob and others, lived a long life full of God's goodness, regardless of their many struggles. This time spent reading the Scripture and praying began to open a new perspective on my healing.

A major turning point occurred when I studied Joshua Chapter 1, which I recommend you start reading for yourself. In this Chapter, God told Joshua emphatically, *"Moses my servant is dead. Be strong and courageous and take over the leadership of Israel."* This is significant because God was literally telling Joshua to put the past behind him and begin to lead. He was saying come on, Joshua; it's your turn to take responsibility. No more depending on Moses. Take on the leadership mantle and run with it. God said in verse 2, *"Moses my servant is dead."* Dead means dead. That era has passed, and now a new dawn is rising along with a new responsibility. There is no time to be stuck in the past, mourning and grieving. Put the past behind you and arise, for God is with you. More importantly, God said He would be with Joshua, just as He was with Moses. As you can imagine, Joshua felt quite inadequate to lead and was deeply saddened by the death of his boss, Moses. He had depended on him in many ways, but now that Moses was not there, it was time to put the past behind him and embrace the new things God had in store.

Yes, I know the future may look bleak without your loved one, but just as God has helped others move forward from their grief both in biblical times and today, He can help you if you allow Him. Like me, you will begin to see things from a different perspective.

As I spent time praying, I realised God had so much to teach me through the pain and trouble I had experienced. As the Bible says: *"When troubles of any kind come your way, consider it an opportunity for great joy." (James 1:2 NLT)*. I began to realise that what you get in a period of pain, you will never get in times of pleasure. Pain is one of God's greatest weapons of change. It can simplify your life, redefine your ultimate focus and give you a real ministry which you earned by experience and not hearsay. When in pain, many are tempted to turn to drugs, give in to their depression or perhaps curse God, but I have consistently proved the only answer that works is the ever-abiding presence of Jesus in the person of the Holy Spirit. He carries you in his arms when you are hurting; cuddles and envelopes you with His unending love. Try spending time in prayer and reading the Bible. See if you begin to experience personal healing and new insight that will show you why the ugly incident you are currently experiencing may have happened. Take a look at this Scripture:

> *"And I will give you treasures hidden in the darkness- secret riches. I will do this so you may know that I am the Lord, the God of Israel, the one who calls you by name." Isaiah 45:3 (NLT).*

When you trust God with the future by taking His Word on board – through reading, meditating and praying – slowly but surely, you will discover that the sad losses the enemy (the devil) used to try and harm you can instead be used as a tool of ministry that will help both you and others.

Chapter 4

MOVING FORWARD

"But one thing I do: Forgetting what is behind and straining toward what is ahead. I press on toward the goal to win the prize for which God has called me heavenward in Christ Jesus." Philippians 3:13b–14.

I explained in the previous chapter how I began to see a different perspective of God's plan for me after several bereavements. Despite this new perspective, the cycle of grief was frequent, especially in the first year of my losses. Several times it felt like I was on an emotional rollercoaster, moving from high and encouraging modes to childlike thoughts, crying myself to sleep and wetting my pillows with tears like David wrote about in the Psalms. There were bad days when I was utterly discouraged and did not want to live.

So how can we move from this emotional state of despondency to regaining our joy and desire to live again? There are no easy answers to these complexities of life. However, God's Word offers us much richness and direction. You will agree that the best person to fix a product is its original designer. For example, you would take a damaged car to a mechanic, not a carpenter. Our original designer and creator, God, made provisions for how we can deal with life's problems in His Word. So, let us explore these truths together.

Allowing Grieving Time

It's okay to cry. Just let the tears flow! Don't bottle it up. Even Christians with strong faith are allowed to cry. This advice was the candid counsel of a dear Christian friend as I grieved the death of my best friend. Today, I am so grateful I listened and allowed the grieving process. This was good for my mental health, and I suggest you take it on board too.

One reason why I love the Bible so much is that it never sugar-coats issues. The biblical stories we read are real human issues that deal with everyday life events. No wonder it's highly recommended as a daily meal that can satisfy our soul. Let's take a look at one humbling event that occurred when a giant of faith experienced a deep and painful loss. Abraham, an icon of faith, lost his dearly beloved wife of many years. You would think this type of man would lift his hands to heaven and say: *"God gives and God takes away, blessed be His name."* Instead, we see him grieving the loss of Sarah, his wife, in Genesis Chapter 23. We read here that Abraham mourned his wife, expressing his grief as men often do at the death of their loved ones.

When we choose not to grieve before we move to the next stage, it may do us more harm than good. Imagine having a bleeding wound on your leg and ignoring it. Your priority would be to stop the bleeding before applying a dressing and a bandage. Afterwards, you would need to rest the wound and allow time for your body to heal. If you don't do this, or if this process is rushed, the pain won't go away because healing may be prevented, and the wound may even get infected, complicating the issue further. Allowing grieving time is like the process I just described. You cannot expect the first year to be easy after losing a loved one.

You need to allow time, give yourself a well-deserved rest and receive reassurance from those God has placed in your life to comfort you. That way, you will be on the path to healing and moving forward from your loss.

Taking Baby Steps

> *"Do not despise these small beginnings, for the LORD rejoices to see the work begin." Zechariah 4:10a (NLT).*

Do not despise the days of little beginnings. What is the Scripture teaching us here, you may ask? It is simply telling us to celebrate any little progress and never take that for granted because it's a sure sign that we are moving in the right direction. Notice what it says – the LORD rejoices to see the work begin. Awesome! It is so good to know that God is pleased when we make or start making gradual progress in recovering from our loss. As I meditated on this Scripture, it painted the picture of a baby learning to crawl and eventually starting to walk. When the baby attempts this the first time, they fall and cry, and their parents reach out to cuddle and comfort them. They never stop the child from attempting this new stage; rather, they clap when the child tries this over and over again. Indirectly, they are encouraging the child to continue in that vein.

Stumbling while learning to crawl is okay. Bad days occasionally happening does not mean you are not yet on the road to recovery. You are making progress. I remember one incident after the loss of my best friend. I had finished working and was walking out of the hospital where I work every day and saw an ambulance pulling in front of me, bringing another emergency.

This triggered an uncontrollable emotion, and I began crying like a baby. It had been several months after the burial of my best friend, and I thought I was making good progress because I was not so tearful anymore, but seeing the ambulance brought back the memory of the bereavement like a movie playing out in front of me. After crying for several minutes, I pulled myself together and heard that comforting voice within me saying, "My daughter, you are making progress regardless."

Triggers that remind you of what you have lost may come in the early stages of grief and in later years. For example, Mother's Day was particularly challenging for my husband in the first few years of our marriage due to his treasured relationship with his late mum. I never had the privilege of meeting my mother-in-law; however, I was told that she was a lovely Christian woman who loved all her children but had a special place in her heart for my husband, who happened to be her last child. Their bond was so deep that her demise left my husband struggling for years prior to our meeting. When we were courting, he often said my Christian character reminded him of his mum. I heard so many good things about his godly mother that I was sad I never got an opportunity to meet her. Basically, Mother's Day in our home became a constant trigger of loss. Having this background knowledge about how such a celebration affected my husband made me extra sensitive in how I handled Mother's Day. This made recovery easier for my husband.

Perhaps you have experienced something similar. A trigger that makes you remember your loved ones in a manner that makes you almost believe you cannot recover from the loss. Believe me; you will. It gets easier every day as you take baby steps and pause to celebrate God's strength and grace through the recovery process. Here's what you do. You sit down with your Bible, open it and begin reading. Or you go for a walk and think about a verse you have memorised. The psalmist wrote this when completely discouraged: *"I lie in the dust; revive me by your word." (119:25, NLT)*. At discouraging times, he knew God's Word had the potential to revive, restore and heal a broken heart. Remember, our God is so merciful that even if our loss has been caused by our carelessness or the consequences of living in an evil world like ours, He is still beside us with compassion amidst our grief. Read the Scripture below meditatively:

> *"For the Lord will not cast off forever: But though he causes grief, yet will he have compassion according to the multitude of his mercies. For he doth not afflict willingly nor grieve the children of men." Lamentations 3:31–33 (KJV).*

Choosing to be Comforted

From what God has taught my husband and I, when we have experienced deep losses like the death of a loved one, we think a great place to begin our recovery process is to choose to be comforted and subsequently healed. You may say this sounds simple because everyone would like to be healed. But, before you make that conclusion, just take a look at this Scripture:

> *"A voice is heard in Ramah, weeping and great mourning, Rachel weeping for her children and refusing to be comforted because they are no more." Matthew 2:18.*

In case you are unfamiliar with this biblical story, every child under the age of two was massacred. We see great loss where mothers are wailing, mourning and grieving so hard that they choose not to be comforted. The Bible clearly states that they refused to be comforted. This was their choice. Remember when I was searching for my glasses? They were neatly tucked away in their case inside my bag. I was so focused on searching for it on the table surfaces that I forgot the possibility that it could be in my handbag. I remember my husband telling me it would be somewhere safe. He tried to remind me to calm down, but in the heat of the moment, I refused, and it was only once I had exhausted my energy that I took a break from searching. Suddenly, I remembered where I kept them. Sound familiar? How could I be so blind?

Believe me; grieving makes us emotionally blind to the fact that there could be better things ahead or more immediate solutions. Once we open our minds to the possibility of a new dawn, we no longer focus on our loss. Instead, we make the wise choice of allowing God to begin the process of healing, comfort and restoration. These solutions can come in several forms. One of the greatest ways God helps our recovery is by providing support systems. Common support systems like family (immediate family or local church) and friends are tools for recovery if we use them appropriately. A word of encouragement or an offer to take away some burden like childcare when a spouse dies are just a couple of ways the Lord graciously brings comfort to the bereaved or people experiencing life's losses. Even if previous friends have moved on or died, God can raise new friendships and give you a new family within the Church. The trouble is that many of us are so stuck in our past that we close our hearts to the possibility that God can bring new people our way. I thought my best friend was gone, but God brought many more friends that filled the role a few years later. The bottom line is by choosing to be comforted, you set the ball rolling on the road to recovery.

Accepting What God Allows

"and had John beheaded in the prison. His head was brought in on a platter and given to the girl, who carried it to her mother. John's disciples came and took his body and buried it. Then they went and told Jesus." Matthew 14:10–12.

"While they were stoning him, Stephen prayed, 'Lord Jesus, receive my spirit.' Then he fell on his knees and cried out, 'Lord, do not hold this sin against them.' When he said this, he fell asleep." Acts 7:59–60.

The two Scriptures above are extracts from two powerful stories in the Bible where God acted differently from how an average human would expect Him to act. The first Scripture comes from the story of John the Baptist, who was Jesus' cousin. He came to prepare the way for Christ, who he described as "One who is greater and whose shoes He is not worthy to untie." After pointing everyone to Him, he was soon beheaded as per the instructions of an angry woman. Why would Jesus allow his cousin to die when he had the power to stop death – particularly such a horrible one? You may like to read the full story in Matthew Chapter 14 before we try to evaluate why God may have allowed this ugly incident.

Mourning

The second Scripture above points us to Stephen who was stoned to death. Why would God allow the stoning of Stephen for simply telling others about Christ when God could have sent thunder from heaven to strike such men? We see this type of deliverance later when Paul and Silas are behind the prison doors (Acts, Chapter 16). A rescue angel from heaven came down and liberated them. Why would God keep quiet in one situation and send deliverance in another? These mind-boggling questions are not straightforward to understand. However, reviewing the nature of God as we learn from the Bible can provide some insight.

God is sovereign and can be trusted to do the right thing for our best interest, even if it is not the outcome we want. To understand this, look at our ultimate example – Jesus. He arrived as a baby, lived until he was 33 years old and died on the cross. To man, 33 years is a very short life. However, to God, this is seen in a different context. We are told in scripture that a day is like a thousand years and a thousand years like a day to God (2 Peter 3:8). This means that God is outside of time and counts differently. To God, 33 years were sufficient for his son to fulfil the mission. The mission that seems so short to us set the stage for the salvation of all men throughout history. This is why we ought to trust God. Perhaps those we are upset about losing have finished their mission, and God wants to open a new chapter.

While writing this, my younger sister lost her 39-year-old husband, leaving behind their little two-year-old daughter. My brother-in-law, being a pastor and a man of prayer, was the last person we expected to die. He was healthy, and on the day of his death woke up to read his Bible. His place of devotion was close to the window, and a riot was going on close by. Sadly, a stray bullet from the riot scene went through the window and hit his chest. He was rushed to hospital. However, he bled and died before any medical intervention was possible. To make this sad loss more difficult to navigate, the police investigation delayed the burial, so it was nine months before he could be laid to rest. Obviously, we struggled as a family to accept this sudden loss. However, the biblical understanding of God's sovereignty made it easier to accept what God allowed. As we mourned this loss, the truths I shared earlier, such as praying, reading God's Word and allowing support from others, made moving forward easier. I am confident these principles can work for you, too, if applied.

Your loss may be more complex than what I have described so far. However, my prayer for you is that you understand that God knows about your situation, and if He allows it, He can be trusted to bring good out of a very ugly situation. I think the serenity prayer sums it up as follows:

> *God, grant me the serenity to accept*
> *the things I cannot change,*
> *courage to change the things I can,*
> *and wisdom to know the difference.* [1]

---

[1] Shapiro, Fred R. (April 28, 2014). "Who Wrote the Serenity Prayer?" The Chronicle of Higher Education.

Chapter 5

HONEST CONVERSATIONS

"Man born of woman is of few days and full of trouble. He springs up like a flower and withers away; like a fleeting shadow, he does not endure." Job 14:1–2.

When I relocated to live and work here in England, I heard people say these words often: "it's your choice," or "it's up to you to do what you like". I heard people even ask children, who have little knowledge about right and wrong, what they would like to do, allowing them to make their own choice at such a young age. I asked work colleagues why people were always given this opportunity without anyone telling them the consequences of their choice. I discovered that one of the main reasons was to ensure it was the individual's choice and not that someone else was influencing them. The problem was that, in most cases, people were too afraid to tell the individual the truth about the consequences of their actions. This approach was different from my African way of making decisions, where parents, friends and even the community will warn you vehemently if you choose to take the wrong step.

While writing this section of this book, it was the seventh day since the beginning of the war in Ukraine, and we had spent the week praying, crying and sometimes watching the ugly

Mourning

events happening between the West and Russia. Surprisingly, I observed that my daughter was already influenced by this news. I noticed her word games that day, and she was spelling all the words she had heard that week. Before that week, she knew nothing about Ukraine or President Putin. As I reflected on these events, I realised that one president's decision was now affecting everyone, including my little daughter's understanding of the world. As my parenting style includes seizing any opportunity to teach biblical or life principles to the children, I knew I had to have an honest conversation with my daughter about the awful things that happen in our world, such as wars and death. Just like I told my daughter, I would also like to have an honest conversation with you. In Jesus' words, *"...you will know the truth, and the truth will set you free."* (John Chapter 8:32).

I believe the most important truth we can tell ourselves is that life is full of trouble. Like the Scripture above says – Man is born for trouble. No matter how much we ignore this fact, death will happen to us and our loved ones. The Bible even went further to guarantee that this is certain:

> *"Yet man is born unto trouble as surely as sparks fly upward." Job 5:7.*

I am confident that honesty, such as telling yourself that your ageing mum may not be here in a few years, is a way of preparing you for the loss when it happens. Likewise, we all know that we live in a fallen world where accidents like plane crashes or medical mistakes happen, which may lead to the death of even a young child. With this in mind, God's Word counsels us to learn valuable lessons from the dead:

> *"It is better to go to a house of mourning than to go to a*
> *house of feasting, for death is the destiny of everyone;*
> *the living should take this to heart." Ecclesiastes 7:2.*

This Scripture simply tells us that we can learn a significant lesson from bereavement. One of the African proverbs in our native dialect says: *"mgbe ina akwa onye nwuru anwu ka i na akwa onwe gi."* This means when you attend the house of mourning, you are getting ready for your own exit. It appears the forefathers who spoke these words of wisdom may have read the biblical injunction in Ecclesiastes Chapter 7:2 above. My husband, who happens to be a priest, often reminds people about this in funeral messages. I believe we should take this sobering thought seriously – *"the living should take this to heart."* Perhaps you have never sincerely thought about your exit from this world. A time of loss and bereavement offers us the opportunity to pause and reflect, which can help us prepare for our own exit.

In the course of dealing with personal bereavements, I learnt that two major things can make moving forward easier: taking steps to prepare for the impact of losses on us and those we leave behind and getting ready for our own exit from this world. Let us explore these two issues one by one.

A Step Ahead: Wisdom from the Ants

> *"Go to the ant, you sluggard; consider its ways and be wise!*
> *It has no commander, no overseer or ruler, yet it stores its*
> *provisions in summer and gathers its food at harvest."*
> *Proverbs 6:6–8.*

Mourning

> *"Four things on earth are small, yet they are extremely wise: ants are creatures of little strength, yet they store up their food in the summer." Proverbs 30:24–25.*

Have you ever heard the popular saying, "I am saving for a rainy day"? This expression portrays planning or saving money for when there is no income or when unforeseen circumstances create more demand than initially anticipated. Once these rainy days come, people use what has been saved to salvage the situation. This is real wisdom. Similarly, the best way to plan for losses is not to wait until it happens but to do this well ahead of time. So how can we plan for great losses like a breakdown in a relationship, loss of personal income or, worse still, the death of a loved one? The scriptures tell us that the principal way to acquire wisdom in life is to fear God:

> *"The fear of the Lord is the beginning of wisdom; all who follow his precepts have good understanding. To him belongs eternal praise." Psalm 111:10.*

The only way to develop a healthy fear of God is by getting to know who He is through His Word, banking on your scriptural knowledge and believing in God's word, knowing it can help you plan for upcoming disasters. We never know what's waiting around the corner; however, we can plan for the unexpected. Remember, God's people are said to perish due to lack of knowledge. If you are knowledgeable about something, it's difficult to be deceived in such areas.

In Sunday school, the story of the two men that built houses was often recounted (Luke Chapter 6:48). On growing up, I realised the nursery story about the three little piggies and the big bad wolf was built on this same biblical principle. Building on a solid foundation by constantly taking in the word of God from the Bible has a way of building your inner self. We are constantly planning for physical things like our retirement, our children's schooling and sometimes for vacations, but many pay little attention to the inner self, which contains our spirit and soul and is the hub of our emotions. If this is not planned for adequately, the danger is that when tragedy strikes, we may become an emotional wreck, stuck in grief and refusing to live again due to a loss that has made us more or less paralysed. Like Solomon, who counselled the lazy man to learn from the ants in the Scriptures above, may I suggest you start planning for losses by reading God's Word and meditating on what it says in these areas, beginning today? That way, your spiritual muscles will be built to handle the emotional strain that comes with losses, helping you bounce back and start moving forward. Moreso, you can read good Christian literature. In addition to frequently feasting on God's Word, the Bible, I spent my leisure time reading books like "When God does not make sense" by Dr James Dobson and "Why Do Bad Things Happen to Good People?" by Melvin Tinker. These books, which were centred on losses, helped me see how I can trust God in challenging times of loss. I am grateful these books were written, as they helped me navigate difficult seasons. I do hope this book will do the same for anyone reading.

Mourning

Ready for Your Exit?

> *"Do not let your hearts be troubled. You believe in God; believe also in me. My Father's house has many rooms; if that were not so, I would have told you. I am going there to prepare a place for you. And if I go and prepare a place for you, I will come back and take you to be with me that you also may be where I am." John 14:1–3.*

The most comforting assurance when bereavement occurs is knowing the deceased person is at peace with God. Jesus' Word in the passage above reassures us that such a person has a resting place in heaven away from the struggles of this present life. With this in mind, it is important to pause and ask yourself this pertinent question: Am I at peace with God? Have you prepared for your exit from this world?

In Matthew Chapter 27, we read about two men who were very near to their own exits. They are popularly known as the thieves on the cross. These two men made different choices when it mattered most. One humbly acknowledged that he deserved what was happening and asked for God's mercy and forgiveness, while the other was proud and arrogant, making a mockery of God. Their attitudes give us a little insight into how people may respond as they near their exit. Some consider thoughtfully that this may be their last chance to ask for God's forgiveness, while others question everything, displaying their arrogance and anger towards God and the world He created. I can assure you that the losses and all the bad we experience are not God's fault but are a consequence of living in an evil world where Satan and his cohorts try hard to make you see God as the enemy. The

Scripture below describes God's gracious attitude towards us, and we would do well to take this to heart:

> *"Seek the Lord while he may be found; call on him while he is near. Let the wicked forsake their ways and the unrighteous their thoughts. Let them turn to the Lord, and he will have mercy on them, and to our God, for he will freely pardon." Isaiah 55:6–7.*

If you have prepared for your exit by responding to God through his son Jesus Christ, congratulations for avoiding the ultimate loss, which we will discuss in the following chapter. Apart from having personal peace with God, it's also important to consider that others around you may not have this same clarity. Are you actively doing what you can with the opportunities you are given to ensure those in your circle exit this world with the assurance they will spend eternity with their maker? If this salient issue is not addressed in life, there is the danger of facing the ultimate loss. What is the ultimate loss, you may wonder? I think exploring it together may help show its seriousness.

Chapter 6

THE ULTIMATE LOSS

> *"Now there was some present at that time who told Jesus about the Galileans whose blood Pilate had mixed with their sacrifices. Jesus answered, 'Do you think that these Galileans were worse sinners than all the other Galileans because they suffered this way? I tell you, no! But unless you repent, you too will all perish. Or those eighteen who died when the tower in Siloam fell on them—do you think they were more guilty than all the others living in Jerusalem? I tell you, no! But unless you repent, you too will all perish.'" Luke 13:1–5.*

While I was gathering the materials for this book, the whole world suddenly started dealing with a pandemic. The loss of human lives around the globe was disheartening. Many were fearful about death and dying. Before long, the Church saw many who would not normally turn to God or go to a church logging into virtual churches for answers. Turning to God in troubled times is always a good idea. However, Jesus had a clear message for those who came to inform him about the two major tragedies displayed in the Scripture above that seemed to occur concurrently. The first is a human political figure causing the death of Galileans, and the second is a natural tragedy of buildings collapsing in

Siloam. Jesus' response to the people that informed him of these sad events should cause us to ponder: *"unless you repent, you will likewise perish"*. Does this mean Jesus does not care that these tragedies happened? The answer is a definite 'no'. Jesus is always close to the broken-hearted (Psalm Chapter 38:18) and binds up those who are hurting (Isaiah Chapter 61:1). However, he drew their attention to the end of all men. Physical death comes to all, and no one can avoid this. The only way out is to escape the final death, which comes from the repentance of wrongdoing, putting our faith in the finished work of the crucified Christ who died for our sins and walking in obedience to God's Word. Only those that choose this part have their names written in the book of life. This is the only way to avoid perishing.

> *"And I saw the dead, great and small, standing before the throne, and books were opened. Another book was opened, which is the book of life. The dead were judged according to what they had done as recorded in the books." Revelation 20:12.*

No matter the loss anyone may face in this life, it can never be described as the ultimate loss. In the grand scheme of things, these losses may be great and grievous, requiring mourning. However, they are still not the ultimate loss. There is a loss that the Bible considers the greatest – the total loss of the soul in eternity. This type of loss cannot be remedied. It is the loss the good Lord wants to ultimately deliver us from, and it remains the most important thing needing our attention. This supersedes our desire to not lose our loved ones, physical health, job and more.

Most people work hard to ensure they do not experience financial loss, and an even greater number of people eat well and exercise to ensure they do not lose their health. We need not mention those who follow the lines of cosmetic surgery to ensure they don't lose their youthful looks. The list of what we do to avoid loss is endless. But pause for a moment and think – have you made preparations to avoid losing the eternal life of joy and peace in heaven? Does that bother you? Don't wait another moment before you make sure this loss is evaded. Knowing that God will judge every man is a really sobering thought that should influence our decision to get it right. Take a reflective look at this Scripture:

> *"And remember that the heavenly Father to whom you pray has no favourites. He will judge or reward you according to what you do. So, you must live in reverent fear of him during your time as temporary residents." 1 Peter 1:17 (NLT).*

I think this Scripture sums it all up, so let's make sure we prepare in a manner that can salvage the ultimate loss. Sorting this issue out guarantees endless rewards, as we will see in the next chapter.

Chapter 7

GRADUATION CEREMONY

As I began writing this book, I attended my MSc graduation ceremony after five years of specialist training. During the ceremony, I was given a certificate confirming that an MSc award had been given to me. Soon after the ceremony, I stared at the certificate for a few minutes while my emotions ran riot. Honestly, that certificate holds a lot of meaning for me and my family. As I gazed at it, the Lord reminded me of the years of struggle and victory at different stages of my training. I remembered that in the second year, we had a surprise pregnancy, and our first baby was on the way. I was so ill that I wanted to quit. I had several emotions running wild – fear, anxiety – and unanswered questions like, "How am I going to cope with all these plates spinning at once?"

My husband gently reminded me why I was doing this training. His words went like this: "Your life is on a mission, and I am here to support you. Soon you will complete these studies and attend your graduation ceremony, so you can't afford to throw in the towel now." These words gave me the energy to continue. I fixed my mind on the end goal – the graduation ceremony and the certificate. As I thought of what I would gain, I stayed on course amidst the challenges. Slowly but surely, five years went by, and my certificate was finally awarded.

Mourning

As I reflected on this, the Spirit of God reminded me that our Christian journey can be like undergoing a long-haul training. Sometimes you feel like quitting because God feels distant, your health is failing, your schoolmates get better jobs or you are yet to secure a livelihood. These life problems discourage you and make you envy those that couldn't care less about our God. Before you give up, may I encourage you as my husband did to me – remember the graduation ceremony in heaven. Whatever challenges you face on this earth are temporal. All losses and grieving are temporal. God is for us and not against us. Jesus, our perfect example, endured this challenging world and died on the cross because he knew this would bring us salvation. Ultimately, when you leave this earth, you will transition to heaven and be with your Father. He will say, "Well done, good and faithful servant." So don't quit now.

I recommend the following Scriptures for your reflection: Hebrews Chapter 12:2, 2 Corinthians Chapter 4:17–18 and Colossians Chapter 3:2–4.

May I end this book with a prayer for you and a few hashtags:

> *Lord, I commit the readers into your loving hands; heal and restore them from their losses. Open their eyes to a deeper knowledge of your son Jesus Christ as they read the scriptures. Help them to move forward from every loss and live again. Ultimately, help them realise that this world is not their home so that we can all live our lives in your will and join you in heaven when our earthly journey is over.*
> *Amen.*

#LossesAreTemporal
#HeavenEternal
#GraduationCeremony
#KeepTheFaith

Another book to read:

New Believers Study Manual

Seven lessons on taking baby steps to grow in faith.

NNENNA MONEME

ABOUT THE AUTHOR

Nnenna Moneme is married to Revd Dozie Moneme, and they currently pastor at St. Paul's Church, Barton, in Newport, Isle of Wight UK, where their core focus is on evangelism and discipleship. As part of their commitment to spreading the knowledge of God's Word, she co-pioneered the DiggingDEEPER biblical content via various social media platforms like YouTube, Spotify, Facebook, Instagram and TikTok.

Nnenna loves reading, writing and serving her husband and children, whom she believes are her primary assignment.

www.ingramcontent.com/pod-product-compliance
Lightning Source LLC
Chambersburg PA
CBHW030046100526
44590CB00011B/339